Stations of the Cross

Mattie McClane

Myrtle Hedge Press

To Rev. James Duc H. Duong

Contents

Stations of the Cross

"Pilate...brought Jesus outside and took a seat on the judge's bench...He said to the Jews, 'Look at your King!' At this they shouted...Crucify Him!' In the end, Pilate handed Jesus over to be crucified."

(John 19:13-16)

Stations of the Cross

Jesus Is Sentenced to Death

I am the witness
of things not right
a woman
in an earth-rocking crowd
colliding elbows
clashing breath
indecipherable noise
Today, sometime
in the future
I watch
and listen
waiting for history
to retell
an ancient story.
Men are elected
they post signs

and run ads
while the rains
flood Texas
It would happen again
the bloodlust
never ended
with thousands
of years
of knowing
the ordained
stand in front
of congregations
the man
the woman
who went to a seminary
who wrote papers
on God
to tell quaint stories
little life lessons

in sermons
in homilies
people pleasers
a little joke
to laugh
before seriousness.
What have we learned
in pews? What
have we picked up
from textbooks?
The world is not
at peace
and a holy
man calls for mercy
the truth is threatened
or erased
the facts denied
we make plans
for what is believed

to be a better place
men of ideas
these political suits
colorful ties
silk pockets
campaign slogans
aimed at winning
it thunders in January
and the locals predict
snow white stuff
within seven days.

It's man-made
climate change
extreme weather
another record
month. I stand where
folks have gathered
for a rally or a trial

Who is innocent
these days? We
have not learned even
while we have
the Scripture
we can recite it
like the alphabet
or prayers
a pledge of allegiance
possibly to sinister men
who no longer pretend
to offer light
their candles'
flames dimly sway
and we stumble
in darkness
in an unhappy gait.
2015 was the hottest year
so go to the beach

in bathing suits
in fashionable bikinis
to rest in the sand
or climb
on granite rocks
where fishermen cast lines
in the rising surf
some ride waves
with gulls around
the ocean is rolling
constant
a slight breeze
the visit complete.

The official's voice
serves interests
pacifying a mob
saying Jesus must die
crucify him

all aren't here
some are in dwellings
on the mountain
or past a blooming field
shaking their heads
in disapproval
the proverbial disapprovers
that done, they go
about business
go to important forums
sit in meetings
chatter in lobbies
they meet Pilate's
decree with silence.
They feel wronged
but go home
to dinners
to public events
where children study

are taught
spelling reading
arithmetic
adding 2+ 2
the people say
they can do nothing.
They can not change
the direction
of the morning sun
beating down
moving from chair
to chair as it rises
waves cannot be altered
they roll forward
and back; the outcome
the sentence
does not change
with wishful thinking
or faint prayers

acceptance is key
dissent is a matter
for the unconnected
for those who live
in the margins
for activists
with nothing
to lose
with light sleep
and the wind blows
rain at the openings
of nooks
and crannies
all day and night
sealed from elements.

The crowd is satisfied
mostly thinking
the happenings are just

the innocent's fortune
is part of the day's news.
How cheap life
has become today
after history, yesterday
when a man healed the sick
raised the dead
and walked on water
experience does not save
the rejected one
who was not interviewed
to be the Savior
of the world.
The story is told
for generations
in pew learning
steadfast followers
who deny the ocean rising
the sun melts

Stations of the Cross

ice sheets
the permafrost
skiers move to other slopes
the man is chosen
for death while
the azaleas bloom
in red, pink, and white,
along a winding road
in a hog automobile
that barely
fits in one lane.

"If a man wishes to come after me, he must deny his very self, take up his cross and follow in my steps. Whoever would preserve his life, will lose it, but whoever loses his life for my sake and the gospel's will preserve it."

(Mark 8:34-35)

Jesus Carries His Cross

The sharp heavy angle cuts
into his shoulder.
This is the fulfillment
of prophecy
that one carries
the weight
of the angry world
people who sleep
in the open
on park benches
while billionaires
are tucked
into bed sheets
others' hunger
prompts stealing
for food

sustenance
the rejection
of the miserable
where poverty
is a crime. No crime
was committed
the mind is focused
on the bruising beam
that wears
into flesh see
obedience
the God
submits to be human
vulnerable
like soft arms
that carries earthen jars
of murky water
and bread
for the children

who do not see
mean spectacles
the structure drags
the flesh bleeds
the sky is gray
with the threat
of rain. The innocent
wonders, aware
in the moment
chaotic voices are heard
all around him. He
thinks he hears
his mother, then
the testosterone commands
of soldiers go in
and out of consciousness
he feels the burden
like he were an animal
with a cruel yoke

laughter intrudes.

The rain pours
throughout the night
on Christmas Eve
in a Southern hub
with nonstop flights
to anywhere
record rainfall
the rivers swell
water travels swiftly
it overflows
its muddy banks
sending water into interiors
the cell phone alarm sounds
flash flood watch

Concerned people talk
about justice

neighbors come out
to see the aftermath
of violence blood
on the ground
from a shooting, folks
looking for answers
looking for community
where citizens gather
everybody says it's too bad
that young people
die, are cut down
in this year of mercy
a holy man prays
asks that others pray
for him. The weight
of the world
is on our God,
he trudges, hearing
that it seems unfair

and someone asks
who is responsible
no one like the quiet
streets, like the house
in the middle
of the subdivision
on a full-mooned night.
This is what happens
when love is abused
red broken bricks
on a downtown street
porous blocks
the white cement
of torture go along
the picture window
the emergency room
where beds roll past
the Savior must
have thought

about prior acts
of believers
of going into common houses
of driving
out demons
simple conversations
with friends, the 12
who watched miracles
were at the baptism
when the Father
sent the Spirit
from heaven
He was pleased
as perspiration rolls
down Jesus' neck.
It is holy water.

In a moment of awareness
Jesus hears a bird sing

nature would seem
to conspire, there is one
that does not. There
is a soft sound
a fluttering take-off
feathers in motion
his lungs heave out air
resolve takes over
in his mind
choices are gone
he must fulfill
go through
with the divine plan.

The high point
across from a river
is where my body trembles
others decide
I am cold

covering my shoulders
fireworks explode
in the sky
colors against black
reflected on water
on a spring evening
music plays
an old time spiritual
swing low
everything is festive
between heaven
and hell the crowd
eats pizza slices
from a downtown vendor
with food trucks
a band of angels
looking after me
on the hill
this is the first time

that I felt his cross.

My Catholic grandmother lived
on a bluff
with a thick line
of uncut grass
with tall seeds
and rising green
with spotted pears
on the ground
beside a highway
where the cars
went fast sounds
of rushing speed
between an embankment
and a pasture
on their way
to the county seat.
She talked

about carrying crosses
the burden
of a common life
when machine shop wages
only stretched
so far when
the husband drinks
and no longer drives
because of an accident
where one was killed.
She raised four children
in a small frame house
until vandals
painted her furniture
with fingernail polish.

Her father gave me
a plastic rosary
and I accepted it like a toy.

I did not then know
how to pray. It is the memory
of the man who also picked
wild blackberries
and carried
them in malt cups
and often stood
at the gravel-scraping
double doors
of a white shed

"But he was pierced for our offenses,
crushed for our sins. Upon him was
the chastisement that makes us whole,
by his stripes, we were healed."

(Isaiah 53:5)

Jesus Falls for the First Time

The burden is too much
The following crowd is convinced
it knows for certain
that the condemned
man is no God
now. Some whisper.
some taunt, feeling satisfied
about judgment weakness
makes people meaner
weakness emboldens
them they embrace
their crime
would vote
for the bully
the one who pushes
others around

and shoves
into positions
calls out opponents
The mob fights
for power
denies the journey
some would find
a champion
in overbearing
voices the rude banter
of onlookers
who worship strength
solid toughness
and would whip a dog.

There is no part
of the bruised bone
that does not sting
burn with weight. My Lord falls,

is counted a failure.
He does not rise above
miserable circumstance
must have no connection
for most think
the blessed
have an easy road.
lean steaks hot soups
the best seats
in the warm house
only good theater
for public men
poll numbers rise
if we are able; there
will be no stumble or fall.

The cross is awkward
the sin too heavy
oil is cheap now

people don't care
about renewable energy.
Grimy fossil fuel
drives a warming world
suppresses the truth
a butterfly in December
designed paper-like wings
land on bushes
out of place
for the season
the missing bees
portend famine
bears walking
on thin ice. We cannot
concern ourselves
most citizens are fed
and satisfied.
Rain hits against
the window

it sounds all night
the now frequent deluge.

Pope Francis calls
for mercy assures us
that God forgives
wrongful deeds
over and over
a thousand times
because of love.

He never tires
of healing men
Jesus is the promise
if we repent
yet oil companies
are not sorry
for the Iraq War
for their part in history

Who will say
the prayers
of penance
for those who bomb
for a commodity
to make profits?

"This child is destined to be the
downfall and rise of many in Israel,
a sign that will be opposed and you
yourself shall be pierced with a sword."

(Luke 2:34)

Jesus Meets His Mother

Mary knew the price
of the immaculate conception
A heart wholly human
breaks for her son
on his path
to a criminal's death
to execution.
Her obedience
is signature
she said yes
to bear a divine child
for God, but now
she prays to the Father
to call it off
Jesus meets his mother

She bore the world's wrong
that day every hunger
every addiction
every lack
a heart mirroring his
own the mother
sees pain
in his eyes
the mocking crown
the mean-spiritedness
of thorns piercing
his forehead.

Nature must weep
for her. The animals stay
close to their nests
they do not venture far
from their young.
Their pity is silence

they do not cry
They have no sound today.

Jesus meets a steady love
like when the electric door
is closed coffee comes
in disposable cups
people gather
in a smoke-filled room
the blue cloud chokes
conversations
meant to pass
the time
a roommate sings in French
then English
about red roses
has a boyfriend
named Harley
or Charlie

the windows are covered
with wire mesh. Sweet
mother's face who
crochets plum-colored throws
for wing chairs
records chicken pox
measles, mumps
in the family Bible
who types letters
to the apartment
with a view
of the foothills.
The wild dream is over.

The sky is heavy purple
cars approach travel
into the coming rain.
The old trees lining
the tobacco town road

are bulging
at the base
are deformed
little branches sway
are blown off
like failed kites
twigs and leaves litter the streets
then the blinding rain.

Mary thinks of childbirth
remember hours
of labor
the pushing
until finally
the infant rests
on her stomach
the beginning
of caring deeply
of worry

of knowing his life
must be extraordinary
his words must be written
down he moves people
to sacrifice luxurious lifestyles
the comforts riches
I am the woman artist
who witnesses
who bleeds
who attests
who creates
like her
so that humanity
can go on
the baby's wet head
short scarlet limbs
belong to the world's Savior.

I sing with my mother's
voice, rich, deep penetration
that cries beyond
our space, beyond our time
into the past.

Jesus saw his mother,
and went on.

"As they led him away, they laid hold of one Simon the Cyrenean who was coming from the fields. They put a crossbeam on Simon's shoulder for him to carry along Jesus."

(Luke 23:26)

Simon Helps Jesus Carry His Cross

My eye now catches
a worker coming
in from a neighboring field
He looks strong,
able to lift the weight
for a line of soldiers
leading Jesus
to his death.
The soldier commands
the passing stranger
to help Jesus,
the targeted politico
the man who rocked
the little boat
who did not go along

with authority
who is counted
as a criminal
Simon is unsure
but he is subject
to enforcers
lifts the cross
is now complicit
with the angry crowd.
The laborer thought
that he had no choice
like citizens
the people
who disagree
with policies
of tyrants
and demagogues
or who would accept
immigrants

who are to be returned
to war-torn countries
lost safety
of thousands denied
and overlooked.
The newcomer
is despised
and unwelcomed
the worn script
has been known
the past
is recited.
I am not telling
any breaking news
no stunning headline
the water floods
the streets swirls
with jutting debris
from former patios

the destruction
of obstacle homes
the pot-hole softness
of broken saturated roads.

"A great crowd of people followed him,
including women who beat their breasts
and lamented over him."

(Luke 23:27)

Veronica Wipes the Face of Jesus

A woman feels compassion
and removes her veil
She, moved by the sight
of suffering, seeks
to soothe
the struggling man.
Veronica wipes his face
from toil burden
the road dirt
dust rising
from a dragged cross
dried and wet blood
from injury. Does she sense
that this prisoner
on his way

to excruciating death
is the Christ
who fulfills prophecy
and gives his life
for an unworthy crowd?
How undeserving
we are common
people fathers
mothers brothers
and sisters
who can watch injustice beckoning
it on. Indifference
is the worst wrong scenes
of a painful circumstance
and we are numb
or hiding out
from daily news
of shootings
in small paragraphs

on the back pages
of newspapers
we are busy
hard unmoved
but in the procession one
goes forward
a story recorded
passed down
on account
of a gesture
of kindness
that is taught
in religion classes
the named woman in history.

The rain taps
against windows.
It comes down for hours
without pause

a car swooshes past
a cloth hanging
from the passenger side
wash it clean remove
meteorologists reports
of extreme weather.
The Scripture
is not unknown to us,
the end
of denial is near
when pretending
falsehood
is ripped away
the man staggers
and there is an imprint
of his face
of the redeemer
on fabric
I am only a witness

in wee hours
when the world sleeps.
I turn on the porch light
to see the evening
it spotlights blown rain.

"Your attitude must be that of Christ...
Though he was in the form a God, he did not
deem equality with God something to be grasp
at
Rather he emptied himself and took the form
of a slave, being born in the likeness of men.
He was known to be of human estate, and it
was thus that he humbled himself, obediently
accepting even death, death on a cross."

(Phil. 2:5-8)

Stations of the Cross

Jesus Falls
for the Second Time

Three soldiers gather
near the fallen man.
They confer wonder
why anyone
would mistake
the weakling
for a God.
They order
say that he must begin
again. They hoist
the cross
onto his small figure
not sturdy
like the legs
that cannot stand

the afflicted drops
to the carpeted floor
calling the name
of a loved one
one spring day
in an Asheville mansion.
The party tours
the grounds
appreciate gardens
tastes wine
from sampling cups.

It is coral calcium
strawberry pie
a fast ride down
the turnpike
firm destiny
in the making nature
is free along a river town

where water turned
the mill's wheel
and fermented brew
belonged to not quite gangsters
but bosses
during prohibition
where stories
are told to children
who defend
their mothers
from thrown lamps
the black dirt
from a potted plant
on a wool rug. I am
the witness
of things not quite right.

The cross is placed
again the burden

the soldiers heckle
him he hears laughter
a low command
to pick up
the pace. He hears
the wooden cross cut
drag scrape
a groove
into the earth
and feels stinging
burning pain
on his shoulder.

He listens for his mother
in a blur of many voices
and craving
any sound
of sweetness, looking
for what

is familiar
his eyes follow his feet.
He cannot hear her now.

"Jesus turned to them and said: 'Daughters of Jerusalem, do not weep. Weep for yourselves and for your children."

(Luke 23:28)

Jesus Speaks to the Women of Jerusalem

Women walk beside
the broken gasping man
he turns his head
to see saddened faces.
He admonishes
the mournful witnesses
of his journey tells
the gathered
not to weep
do not cry for me
not to beat
their breasts
in protest. "Pray
for yourselves

and your children,"
he tells the women.

These are the women
of first histories
early records
who feel
for the injured
whose hearts
reach out
in compassion
to the innocent
to the abused
and wrongly condemned.
Christ's pain
did not escape
their senses
or eyes telling
all on the dark day

they were present
at the sham trial
following fate
of a gentle prisoner
a man who had healed lepers
and prayed
for the poor.

The circumstance
of women
yesterday, today
is from brutish lessons
on vulnerable flesh
famous strife
in paper books
primary sources
that tell
about battles coups
the whims

of violent men
who sit in legislatures
endlessly talking
about rights
of the unborn
while they beat
the world's girls
into submission
with edicts
and lawful decrees.

Oh women, take pity
heavy downpours
armed oppressors
the great mistakes
political decisions
church traditions
maddening hierarchies
that exclude

half populations
and rock
unsettle
silent generations
with sanctioned wrongs.

"I am like water poured out;
all my bones are racked... my throat
is dried up like baked clay. My tongue
cleaves to my jaws; to the dust of death
you have brought me down."

(Psalm 21:15-16)

Jesus Falls for a Third Time

His small body
is overwhelmed
cannot stand
his bleeding head
under lumber
red tinged curls
ringlets stiff
under crushing
weight weary eyes.
Soldiers curse
at the beaten life;
their job
is not easy. The man
should be tougher
on his way
to execution

he should have more fight
not collapse
they lift struggling flesh
to his feet
the knees sway
he trips forward
a little farther
up along the rising dirt path.

The following crowd
seems confused
for a second wonders
about the pathetic scene
Mary bears
her son's agony
his painful fail
she wants to go
to him but soldiers push
her back. God knows

his plan perfect
of divine obedience
resolve to complete
the journey
to a foretold end.
Prophets describe
the passion
in stories
and the rain comes
down in another city
in another time
after salvation
when people plead ignorant
about the toll
that has not been hidden.

Everyone professes
that love
conquers angry

men jealous
of rivals
kick-in ribs
break ankles
with black boots
or whatever footwear
the local villain
wears sports memories
in night dreams
waking the mind
to yesterday.

I read news articles
I am the witness
of corporate greed
that hides truth
with quack scientists
who pollute oceans
roast the air

where pelicans fly
in the morning looking
for schools. I see
the electronic ballot
switch votes
and know
a poll tax
on God-given rights.
I hear the rain blow
swirling waves
against glass.

My mother reads
about Fatima
the children's vision
she dwells
on the seals. What
can it mean
for a world in turmoil?

The woman
a New Windsor prom queen
with lifelong
night dreams
of apocalyptic desolation. She prays
that her family
will taken up
in the rapture
to snickers
and dismissal
and a politician wins
an election. The rain pours.
She is alone
with a television
in a mint-green bedroom
and a Christian
friend who cleans
her house
does laundry

and leaves money
for her birthday
on the kitchen table.

"We should not tear it. Let us throw dice to see who gets it." (The purpose of this was to have the Scripture fulfilled. "They divided my garments among them, for my clothing they cast lots")

(John 19:24)

Stations of the Cross

Jesus is Stripped of His Garments

The uncovering
of a brutalized captive
the injury
from lashes
marked torn flesh
wine-colored wounds
everyone can see
the result
of hatred
the actions
of hot mindless crowds.
When the clothes
are taken,
it is revealed
yet only women

the mother sees
knows with her heart
the damage
of the damning mob
ugly disclosure
no holding back
no more hiding
the truth
of human cruelty.

Jesus knows his fate
he is the ransom
like when souls combined
into a concentration
of the sin felt
seen during services
in another time
all mischief contained
in the body

when music played
and the impact
was palpable
the shock real
electrifying sensation
in the basement
where choirs practiced
in the chapel.

"When they came to Skull Place, they crucified him there and the criminals as well...

(Luke 23:33-34

Jesus Is Nailed to the Cross

The breaking
of bone
sounds of hammers
one criminal
is to the left
another to the right.
Our Lord
is crucified
in front
of a following crowd.
Did anyone watch
the pain
and attempt
to free him? The
Christ said, "Forgive
them, for they not what

they're doing." A man
so tortured
let them off. He
did not blame
or cast a stone
not interested in who
was guilty
time goes by
and we now recognize
the story
etched in
the mythos
repeated
for centuries
in the best places
so professed
for countless generations
in cathedrals
in country churches

where people kneel
with sacred words
on raspberry lips.

The poet's imagination
is faulted
for retelling
the Scripture.
A long poem
cannot convey
sacred meanings.
I pray but do not
know or suffer
like Christ.
The poet
is a wordsmith
a truth-seeker
but only guesses
when conveying

the divine plan,
a plan for the ages
of eternal things
that never go out
with time. Yet the crowd's
anger is not gone.
They have not loved
the rising oceans
the pelican
on its spiral dive
or the chatty gull.

"When noon came, darkness fell
on the whole countryside and lasted
until mid-afternoon. At that time,
Jesus cried in a loud voice… 'My God,
my God, why have you forsaken me?'"

Stations of the Cross

Jesus Dies on the Cross

Jesus thirsts for water.
is given vinegar
His senses feel little
are numb; he dreams
of green fields
in the springtime
he is aware of pain
in moments. He hears
the voices of women
of soldiers. Moisture builds
in the sky, the sky
becomes heavy violet
he labors to breathe
cannot take
in a full breath.
He is aware

of his mother's
presence he looks
down at the crowd.
Christ knows
that it is almost over
he struggles, draws
in air. Clouds hide
the sun. Jesus again
asks for water. He hears
rumbles of thunder
the people begin
to scatter going back
on the trail
to their homes
the rain washes
his face
in lines streaks
the sweat
the blood

Stations of the Cross

from his forehead
dirt rolls away
in tiny streams
from his arms
"My God, My God
Why have you forsaken me?"
His head drops
to his chest. It is done.

"As it grew dark… Joseph from Arimathea arrived—a distinguished member of the Sanhedrin… Then having brought the linen shroud, Joseph brought him down.

(Mark 15:42-46)

Jesus is Taken Down from the Cross

A group brings the linen
to take Jesus' body
from the cross.
The crowd has left
they have other concerns
now the evening menu
they hear
from wise men
who cannot remember
the commotion
that will only
come back
in dreams, how the sky
turned lavender

then indigo how
the rain pounded
the earth until every blade
and petal
was bent over
crushed
from tears.
The great thirst
could not be quenched
the people stood
by deep wells
with dry dippers
water flooded
the streets
in another time,
water rising
into living rooms. Water
everywhere, covering

the towns, the market making
them appear
as rivers and seas.

"They took Jesus' body and in accordance with Jewish custom bound it up in wrappings of cloth and perfumed oils. In the place where he was crucified there was a garden...they buried Jesus there..."

(John 19:40-42)

Jesus is Laid in the Tomb

The story is familiar
so we experience
no alarm
or shame
we are assured
of mercy
promised forgiveness
salvation
in three days
smokestacks cloud
the sky. Did Jesus die
for corporations
for the bottom-liners
for drillers
and spillers
that cover

the pelican
with a suffocating fluid
for those who want profit
more than sustained life
on the planet?

Lamb of God
who takes away
the sins
of the world
have mercy on us.

Lamb of God
who takes away
the sins
of the world
have mercy on us.

Lamb of God
who takes away
the sins
of the world
grant us peace.

Neighborhood deer
eat white roses
in the middle
of the night
they cut the tender buds
and I sigh
considering
a loss
of extraordinary beauty.
the bushes
are left
the flowers
will come again.

Jesus is Laid in the Tomb

Index of Bible Verses

About the Author

Mattie McClane (Kristine A. Kaiser) is an American novelist, poet, and journalist. She is the second and youngest daughter born to James L. and Shirlie I. Myers in Moline, Illinois. Her father was a commercial artist and her mother worked as a secretary.

McClane's earliest education was in the Catholic schools. Her experience with their teachings deeply affected her. At a young age, she became aware of gender inequality. She credits her early religious instruction for making her think about "all kinds of truths" and ethical matters.

McClane's parents divorced when she was eight years old. Her mother remarried attorney John G. Ames and the new couple moved to a house beside the Rock River. The river centrally figures in McClane's creative imagination. She describes her childhood as being "extraordinarily free and close to nature."

McClane moved to Colorado and married John Kaiser in 1979, in Aurora, just East of Denver.

They then moved to Bettendorf, Iowa where they had three children. John worked as a chemist. Mattie became interested in politics, joining the local League of Women Voters. According to McClane, she spent her 20s "caring for young children and working for good government."

She graduated from Augustana College with a B.A. degree in the Humanities. She began writing a political column for Quad-Cities Online and Small Newspaper Group, based in Illinois.

Her family moved to Louisville, Kentucky where she continued with her journalism and then earned an M.A. in English from the University of Louisville. Critically acclaimed author Sena Jeter Naslund directed her first creative thesis, "Unbuttoning Light and Other Stories," which was later published in a collection.

She was accepted to the University of North Carolina at Wilmington's M.F.A. in Creative Writing Program, where she wrote the short novel Night Ship, working under the tutelage of Pulitzer Prize winning author Alison Lurie. McClane studied with Dennis Sampson in poetry also. She graduated in 1999.

She would write a column for the High Point Enterprise in North Carolina. She would later write for the News and Observer. McClane has regularly published commentary for over 25 years.